THE T

SHALL blossom

CW01512692

The Desert Shall Blossom

Poems for the journey from Ash Wednesday to Easter Monday

Janet Killeen

wild goose
publications

www.**ionabooks**.com

First published 2025 by
Wild Goose Publications
Suite 9, Fairfield, 1048 Govan Road, Glasgow G51 4XS, Scotland
A division of Iona Community Trading CIC
Limited Company Reg. No. SC156678
www.ionabooks.com

ISBN 978-1-80432-369-4

Cover photo © Porechenskaya | Dreamstime.com

Overseas distribution
Australia: Willow Connection Pty Ltd, 1/13 Kell Mather Drive,
Lennox Head NSW 2478
New Zealand: Pleroma, Higginson Street, Otane 4170, Central Hawkes Bay

Printed in the UK by Page Bros (Norwich) Ltd

CONTENTS

INTRODUCTION

'The wilderness and the dry land shall be glad, the desert shall rejoice and blossom.'

Isaiah 35:1 (NRSV)

The steps are slow and challenging between Ash Wednesday and the beginning of Holy Week. Time for reflection in Lent to explore the Temptations of Jesus and the experience of Wilderness. Calvary is more than three years away, yet how powerfully the temptations anticipate the events of that intense week.

Suddenly the pace accelerates, and we travel from Jericho to Jerusalem and the cheers and anticipated triumph of Palm Sunday and the ensuing days of mounting conflict and, for the disciples, uncertainty and perplexity. And then it is Friday, and the agonised steps of the Via Dolorosa.

For centuries Christians have found meaning in the Stations of the Cross. Although there is no foundation in the Gospels for several of the traditional stations I feel they have great significance. The power of the imagination – what the poet Keats called 'the Truth of the Imagination' – is to bring experience to life and enable us to enter in, to participate and respond. For centuries, devoted pilgrims have accompanied the steps of Jesus, pausing alongside these imagined stages of his walk to the cross. So I have used some of the stations as a way of imagining the unimaginable. I've also tried to use a variety of voices and perspectives to bring us nearer, perhaps, to the events of that journey, to the long hours of waiting on the Sabbath and then to the amazing, at first unbelievable, revelation of an empty tomb and the dawning reality of Resurrection.

The Days of Lent

Ash

Fell on Valentine's Wednesday that year.
A strange configuration of
Repentance and Romance.
Facetious or profound,
A heart, drawn on the brow in ashes,
Goes beyond solemnity to the joyous laughter
That fills eternity,
And beyond all sorrows
Borne on the cross.
Love, whether scribed in curves or right angles,
It is, perhaps, all one.

BREAD

Holding the stone, he might remember
The vast millennia of its formation.
The jostling of tumultuous seas
That smoothed and soothed the sliding rocks,
Compressing, shaping to this perfect oval
Satisfying to the hand.
Sun-warm, a loaf of stone. But
Hard as the rock-strewn path that lay ahead.

Perhaps he shared the helpless hunger of a child:
Generation after generation
Of famine and failed harvest,
The desperation of the mother,
Her body's drought of everything but love.
Or foresaw how the hungry might be fed:
A gathered crowd,
The broken bread and fish
Passed out among them until all had eaten.
But not all. Not all the endless aching hungers
Yet to come.

Saw too, and knew
Within his racked and famished body's core,
That one day he would take bread
And share it with his friends.
A gift of love. Only for him,
The bread he gave to them would be as stone,
Hardened and sullen with betrayal:
The one he called a friend
Ate it and went his way,
And it would be an end, as this
Was a beginning.

Perhaps he saw beyond the horror
Of that evening and the long-drawn day
That was to come. He might have seen
A road between
The hills, the dust stirred by the feet
Of travellers. Heard their eager questioning
And welcome to their home.
And knew how he would take the bread again,
Oval and soft, with untold millennia
Of healing yet to come, of consolations

Enough for all the hungry and the wronged,
The grieving and the weary. He would take the bread
And break it for their brokenness,
And they would know him.

Matthew 4:3 & Luke 4:2–4

DOMINION

Poised at the rim of the world,
Sensing beneath his feet
Its slow turning, night and day, night and day.
Days melting into years
And into centuries, millennia,
As kingdoms rise and fall.
All the glory and glitter of wealth,
The plunder of empires,
Slaves and subjugated peoples
Led in processions of chains.
Arches glare, triumphant in marble,
Burning the eyes in sunlight,
Gardens and fountains, peacocks,
Prisons, roads, walls, cities,
Factories, plantations,
Voyages of conquest,
Crusade and captivity, and always
The trampling march of armies.
All, all
Rise and fall, rise and fall
And their riches turn to dust.

Emperors and kings,
Czar and Führer and President,
Defy mortality a little
Yet each one drops alone into the pit of history,
To be forgotten.

Standing at the rim of the world,
Time turning beneath his feet
As power and glory
Parade before him in all their fleeting glamour
Borne on the backs of the poor and the enslaved,
'I will not', he said. Only love. Only willing worship,
Only servanthood can build a kingdom.

Luke 4:5–8/Matthew 4:8–10
(Luke places this temptation second in his account.)

HEIGHTS

There may have been laughter,
The faint, gentle mirth of angels
Who'd seen a greater fall than this.
An unimaginable fall from dizzying heights
Of splendour, down, down through planes of light
Invisibly to earth,
To form and substance, to this frail coat of flesh
We call humanity, and wear so brief a time
Until mortality claims us.

So, poised upon the utmost pinnacle of the Temple,
The city streets and alleys far below,
The scurrying figures, indistinguishable
Yet infinitely precious,
The breeze quickening in the upper air,
The wakening sun dancing in the mists
Rising from the far fields,
Perhaps he also laughed. 'I have already fallen,'
He might have said. 'Fallen from the furthest zone
Of uncreated light to earth, and angels sang
To greet me.

I have no need of rescue, no miraculous
Intervention to stun the crowd and take their choice away.'

Even in my last mortal hours, he knew,
I can ask for legions of angels swift to rescue me,
To carry me on their hands
Back to the throne of heaven,
And leave all undone here.
But there is a height to climb
With pierced feet and torn and tortured hands
And the same temptation: prove yourself,
Come down from the cross and show the crowd.
Call up the angels, rebuke your enemies,
Declare yourself incontrovertibly Son of God.

And from the awful vertigo of the cross,
Three years from now,
The same strong answer will be given.

Matthew 4:5–7/Luke 4:9–12

Between Beasts and Angels

Imagine how it might have been for him
When, as darkness gripped the stones, they came.
Feather and scale, fur, hoof, claw, paw and limb,
Crawling, or lithe, a rush of wing; now tame
And innocent. The scorpion held aloft
Its deadly curl of death; the wild ass
And jackal came together and the soft
And stealthy lynx crept close, eager to pass
Within this wide circumference of grace.
Who knows whether at breathing night they slept
Beneath the arch of piercing stars, each place
Still and without harm, while angels leapt
Amazed, delighted, seeing how these wild
Enmities are by this Man reconciled.

Mark 1:13

TURNING TOWARDS JERUSALEM

JERICHO

No trumpet-triumph now,
No crash of conquest,
Walls collapsed in dust and terror,
No slaughtering entry
Ravaging men, women, child and beast.
    Instead, a crowd, eager, curious
    Jostling to glimpse
    With desperate hope:
    Recognition, status, longing, need,
    Confused and buzzing in a confluence
    Of cries and calls.
A history forgotten,
Or if remembered, only as heroic,
Its horror veiled
And, surely, long ago,
The rubble buried, overgrown.
Only the scarlet cord of Rahab
Stretches through the centuries,
Saving and salvaging
Within the true King's genealogy.

And so a beggar, besieged by blindness,
Elbowed in the crush (all
Greedy for a view of this man Jesus,
Each one mouthing, a prophet. A king. A healer.
Could he be 'the long-awaited?')
Takes hold of Rahab's cord
And cries out,
'Have mercy on me, Son of David!'
Refusing to be silenced.
And cries out still,
'Have mercy on us, Son of David!' Cries
From the silenced mouths of every victim
Besieged by poverty, or war, or terror.
Above the restless tumult of our time
The true King hears,
And he will call them to his presence,
Naming each one, a Son of Honour,
Prized and unforgotten.

HOLY WEEK

PARADE

On a dais, the self-proclaimed god
Rivals the scant sunlight.
Breast encrusted, sashed,
Honours terrestrial, dominions
Conquered or claimed.
Rank upon rank of high-stepping soldiery,
Swivel and snap to acknowledge him.
The dull sheen and weight of missiles
Lumber on vast-wheeled carriers;
Tanks grind by, their turrets turning,
Gun barrels phallic in salute.
And the hypnotised crowd
Sways as one, in adulation.

*

While on a street, not far,
Perhaps almost parallel,
An alley of the old town,
Deserted by once-captivated crowds,
Silence falls, and the dust stirs
As the wind is blowing
As it will.
A man on a donkey rides
Carefully, gently,
Towards eternity, showing
    It could be otherwise.

THE TEMPLE COURTS

The week began with rage, rage
In the Temple court, the tables thrust aside,
Coins spinning into dust, animals
Bleating and scampering
Down streets and alleys, scenting
The breath of life.
Pigeons, uncaged, taking to air
In swirls of gladdening flight.
The money changers, traders in sacrifice,
Cowering as whips of words scoured them,
And religious leaders storing up those words
To turn against him. 'My Father's house.'

Yet even then, when heat and light bore down
On him, and he was ringed with crowds,
Eager, curious, grateful,
Waiting for a miracle, and at their centre
Such hostility, ravenous for error,
A blasphemy, a spike on which he could be hung,
Even then, he turned with tenderness

To see the woman slip unnoticed
To toss her livelihood with love
Into the treasury chest.

It was as if the hills around Jerusalem
Drew closer, pressing in
With thunder riffling always at their backs
As though to stifle us with heat,
Cramping and caging us,
And at their core, a man locked in conflict,
One after another, questions, questions,
Traps and snares, baited and poisoned
With malice.
We watched, yet not seeing,
Not understanding, how deadly were their words,
How short the days now left to us,
How perilous the path he walked.

THURSDAY

FOR THE JOY THAT AWAITED HIM

Once, before time, before any need of form
Or measurement, or name
(All being known in joyous love and oneness)
Dwelling in darkness, richer than the core of the sun,
More dazzling with radiance, brilliant
With the passionate mysteries dreamt in the mind of God.
Life, brimming with abundance, far beyond
The unknown, waiting depths
Of seas or forests, still uncreated and unnamed.
A ceaseless celebration,
An endless delight of inexpressible glory,
A jubilation of angels.

Then (and who knows when?) the choice, the risk:
To make known, reveal, a form, a Being
Comprehensible to faith, with all its possibility
Of love and reciprocity.
And all its possibility of loss.

A Word spoken: a Word that upholds
Universes, dimensions of space,
Pathways of stars exceeding all imagination.

Then, the naming of an unfolding creation.
Calling it into form and presence:
Time, space, substance, light.
Dark. Day. Stars, sun, moon, night.
Fern and tree, grass, flower, fruit.
And creatures of gait and flight and fluid motion.
Then, Man and Woman.

*

And all things subject now to time,
In the eternal watchfulness of the sustaining Word,
To choose again: to lay aside that form of God
(Ignored, rejected or at the best, faintly perceived and
barely understood)
And enter through the confining womb,
And narrow gate of birth, to show in human form
Through thirty years,
The true and loving, patient nature of Himself.

And in the last acts of love,
To hold and wash with tender carefulness
The hardened, grimed and weary feet of friends
(His own unwashed),

And tear the bread and offer wine
For their refreshment.
And hear, so soon, how their feet fled from him,
As his captors trampled the quiet garden.
Then (he who is Word and Life) kept
Silent in the face of lies,
And the unrelieved torment of sun-darkening death.

Sleep

I slept. And now I cannot sleep,
Haunted by the mockery of cockcrow.
Remembering that boast, my tears
Fall like stones.
Remembering too all our shuffling protests,
Not me, not me, surely not me.
The meal's mystery
A horror to us, of blood offered
Against every instinct of zealously
Observed Law.
Then the darkening garden
And his plea for friendship. Stay
With me, stay with me,
And he walked away
A little way, to pray. We slept,
Unaware of what was being
Wrestled out alone. Only when we saw him
Returning to us, gaunt, exhausted,
Weighed down with sorrow,
Only then did we see our sleep as a betrayal,
Piercing his heart as surely as the thorns and nails
That followed.

Then the dark and quiet garden splintered
Into shouts and the trudge of armed men,
Torches, flaring on our faces,
A kiss,
And my slashing folly of a sword-stroke.
We fled, the dread of it on us, each one to hide,
Even I, insistent in my boasting, denying him.
Then the cock crowing. And my heavy tears,
Falling like stones.
Only the women stayed with him
Throughout that day of darkness. I had seen men
Pinned against the sky to writhe and die.
Horror and shame kept me away.
Twelve, now eleven, we clung together through that day
And through a restless Sabbath, yet
Each one was alone, ashamed, afraid.

I cannot sleep.
Wait and watch, he said.
And now we wait, and watch, sleepless.
Waiting for cockcrow, waiting for daybreak,
And a faint shivering hope of a new dawn.

THORNS

The show trial limped wearily through the night.
False witnesses, stumbling over one another
To earn their fee. The soldiers bored and restless,
Religious and politicians smug in their expediency,
Shrugging off the horror
Of their judgement. A temporary alliance.
The gaping crowd now drifts away
To wineshop, gossip, darkened streets
And the huge indifference of other lives.

He is alone, despite encircling faces:
Moments of waiting
Before the torment begins, and then it breaks on him.
The mockery of kingship, the robe and reed,
    the agony of flogging.
And one man, young perhaps,
Desperate to prove himself a man,
Not old enough to know the endurance of pain
Only the casual cruelties that make your fellows laugh.
One man rips a bush out of the ground,
Twisting thorns, thick as thumbs, into a crown.
Laughing, the company of them, bored,

Half-dreading the brutality of their duty,
Laughing, they thrust the circlet onto his head,
Watching the blood spurt out and trickle thickly
    down his face.

What crown was given him?
The kingdoms of this world,
The costly weight of government,
The tyrannies and abuse of power.
Kingdoms held together by oppression
Or dismembered by greed.
All earthly power was crushed upon his head
With all its pain and sorrow.
And from his cross he saw and bore the slow millennia
Turning. Empires rising and falling, conquest
And dominion.
It was Adam's curse that crushed him,
Thorns and servitude, hard labour,
Serfdom, slavery, gathered into a mockery of a crown,
And borne with patient and unfailing hope.

Slow Steps to the Cross

Jesus Falls the First Time

Stones, more brutal than a boxer's knuckles,
Rose up to smash and graze his knees,
His battered feet.
Did he hear, in that moment of falling,
Ironic laughter, echoing down the years of ministry
'Lest you dash your foot against a stone'?
Falling, with all the haplessness of childhood,
Falling beneath the heavy cross beam
That jarred and crushed his shoulder and his neck.
Outspread hands, that could not save him
From his fall, our fall, the desperate vulnerability
Of his fully owned humanity.

Not all the legions of angels, nor
His own divinity
Could spare him this, his choice
To enter fully into our frail nature

And say, 'This is my body'. This flesh
Of bone and nerve, of pain and nakedness,
Of blood, tears and sweat, thirst and hunger,
And now of weary agony,
This body, enduring all, incorporating all
Into himself.
There were no angels here to bear him up,
Just the rough wrenching of a legionnaire's grip
To set him on his feet again and smite him forwards.

JESUS SEES HIS MOTHER

She, held roughly back by soldiers guarding the route,
He, stumbling forward,
Blind with acid sweat and blood,
Their eyes meeting, no touch, no embrace,
No words. They would come later.
All the love and the shared pain, of more than thirty years,
Leaping between them in that meeting.
Did she remember then,
The sword that would pierce her heart
Spoken of so long ago
And wrenched within her so terribly now?
She knew this destiny he had chosen to fulfil,
Had glimpsed it often, even in his childhood,
Remembering her own calling to give him birth
And the cost of that, stigma and terror,
The sharp straw on which she laid him,
The weary churning dust of the roads,
Asylum seeker in Egypt. And the fear of Herod.

She knew his power to change the water into wine,
Even then recognising
That this was no easy miracle

But would one day be fulfilled at the cost of his own blood
To make the wine of life.
She knew too, a carpenter's wife,
The exact nature of his dying
Against the splintered wood,
And the nails, wedges of rough iron,
And the heavy mallets that would drive them home.

Who knows his thoughts?
His pity and compassion for her
Standing so bravely alone
To watch his journey and be with him at its close,
Even as she had been with him at its earthly beginning.
His gratitude, that even to that dreadful end,
Despite bewilderment and deep distress,
She had not swerved away from serving him,
Loving him, and even now, if she could enfold him
In the safety of her own body she would do so.
And yet, knowing as she did what was the greater love,
Releasing him,
That all things might be made new.

Veronica Wipes the Face of Jesus

Mark her, as she thrusts forward,
Her hands stretched out, the cloth, wet with tears
As well as water,
The soldiers, touched perhaps with sudden pity,
Letting her slip between them
To see her take such simple love,
Such a simple gift, a moment's refreshment,
To wipe away the terrible travail of his journey.
Who knows the truth of the legend? Yet
All would wish they could have found such courage
To press forward and be a part
Of this most agonised of roads. She, bearing the image
Wiped from his face in sweat and blood,
Holding in her heart the face, familiar then
But unseen now, and showing us how tenderness
Reveals his countenance in acts of kindness,
Captured in those lineaments of grace.
Revealing to us how the suffering Christ is seen
In all the faces of the destitute and tormented,
The abused, the persecuted and the refugee,
The crushed and rejected
That are the true ikon of his likeness.

THE TREE'S SONG

Along hushed streets,
The crowd aghast, the stones silent,
Yet the wood grain sang to him.
> (The weight of government crushed across
> His shoulder, rough and splintering,
> Jarring against the thorns.)
The wood sang to him:
'You saw the seed fall into darkness
From the tree's height,
A fall, alone, a dying.
Until the earth split as
Leaves unfurled in tenderness:
A stem, a sapling, thrusting skywards
Through thirty years of growth.

'You know the touch of wood
Planed and caressed to light,
Grain enlivened, smoothed and ready,
Not this, rough and ribbed,
Cut down in haste
And sawn for bloody purpose.'

(Still the grain sang to him,
Each step accompanied
By the deep silent thrumming of the wood.)

'And after, thrown down
And shamed, we will be fuel
Taken by stealth tonight for some poor man's fire,
Our breath given for warmth,
For light and comfort.
So, another song.

'As you too will be cut down,
And all your dreamers will see only death.

'But you will rise:
As timber to uphold the sky,
Light breaking in brilliant leaf,
A flame to burn
In unimaginable
Hearths and hearts.'

Jesus Meets the Grieving Women of Jerusalem

If we had ears to hear, we might have heard
The stones cry out. Not in worship
But in horror that such suffering should stumble
Over them. Such cruelty, such ruthlessness,
Here in Zion, the beloved city.
But the ancient stones are mute,
And the crowd, fenced in by soldiery,
Has fallen silent now. The mob, hired
To jeer for his crucifixion, has slunk away,
Their voices shamed to silence.
The disciples, too, in agony of thought,
Have hidden away, their world undone.

But there, linked by love and a defiant courage,
The women force their way past an unnerved soldiery,
Women who had followed him from Galilee,
Women who have gathered from the courtyards and streets
Of Jerusalem, melded in their shared distress,
Their tormented hands, moving in ancient,
    ritualised gestures,

Their tears, flowing as though deep had called to deep
To release the hidden springs.
And now he sees them, pauses, turns,
Straightening the torn back,
Looking through bruised and blurred eyes
To see these clustered, despairing women
And take their pain into himself.
As he does so, it seems as if the world stops,
Guttural commands fall silent, the murmur of the crowd
Dies away, and there is only their terrible grief
And his voice.
'Do not weep for me. Do not weep for me.'
It is yourselves and your children who will bear
This unspeakable cost. You will say then that women
Are blessed who have not borne children,
Who do not fear the terrible vulnerability
Of women and their babies
Under siege.
I would have offered sanctuary, O Jerusalem,
But you could not recognise me.
And now weep, not only for yourselves,
But for all those in the centuries to come
Who will be helpless in the cruel hands and ambitions

Of warlords, of besieging princes who hate peace
And lust for power.
The countless women and children, who become
The spoils of war.
Weep for them.
And he saw the dreadful unravelling
Of kindness at the heart of history.

Weep, women of Jerusalem, weep
For Palestine and her mothers,
For Yemen's children, for the slaughtered women
Of Bosnia, for girls stolen in Nigeria,
Raped in the Republic of the Congo,
For child soldiers, deceived into cruelty,
For young women trafficked into Britain,
For women and girls in Afghanistan
And Sudan.
Weep not for me, he said, knowing
All the anguish that lay ahead, yet the hope of resurrection,
Which in its time will make all things new
And heal the tears of the world.
Weep not for me, but add your tears to the balm
That will bring justice to the oppressed,

Restore the kinship of humanity,
And consolation
To the broken minds and bodies
Wrecked and racked by time.

If we have ears to hear,
The stones, aghast, are weeping now,
Crushed beneath the indifferent feet
Of generations.

JESUS FALLS FOR THE THIRD TIME

The crowd is silent now. And we too,
Looking on across two thousand years,
Are silent. This most terrible helplessness,
This stumbling walk, and then the trip
(So small a thing, so small a word), a stone
That sends him full length to the ground,
Bloodied and bruised. No part of him now
That has not shuddered with the pain
Of wounds and torment.
Three times, like us, unable to save himself,
Flung down against the slabs and dust
Of this, his mortal journey.
We watch the slow levering up
From hands, knees, feet to walk again,
The unrelenting thrust of the soldiers
Who force him on; the dragging steps; yet
The fixed will that sets his face towards Golgotha.

How can the earth bear the heaviness of this disaster?
The Creator descends to earth, not heralded by angels

But abandoned, isolated, broken. Surely the rocks
Should split, the city tremble?
But no threat or blame, no word of judgement.

Surely he said, 'My yoke is easy and my burden light'?
But this is an intolerable load,
The grief and pain of our humanity,
The ruin of all our falls and brokenness,
And only he can bear it for us.
And as he falls three times,
So he will rise on the third day, and rising unencumbered
Lift us up.

STRIPPED OF HIS GARMENTS

As he was born into the world,
Naked except for blood and the waters of birth,
So now they stripped him,
Drawing on that age-old sense of shame,
That vulnerability and exposure.
And while they gambled for his garments
Did they pause to contemplate
That seamless robe and wonder
At the love and skill that would have made it for him,
At the terrible contrast of his helplessness
And the devotion that it showed?
And as they diced for his death
Did they hear the words of forgiveness?
That extraordinary gift releasing them, and everyone
Involved in the trial and the horror of it,
From the dread and blame of generations
Who would demand wrath and persecution
As though they held a mandate
For the judgement of God.

And now exposed, most fully revealing
The incarnate presence of God,

The flesh in which he had glorified God
Full of grace and truth.
Now, for those who could see,
God was naked before them,
At one with all the generations of humiliation,
The shame of the woman dragged before him
   in the Temple court,
The thousands of his fellow Jews
Naked before their murderers at Babi Yar.

Most truly one with us,
Love and mercy, words of grace and healing,
Revealed in the extremity of his pinioned limbs,
His battered, weary body.
Was it this that caused the officer to exclaim
'Truly this man was a son of God'?

MATES TO DIE FOR

'Mates at the "Mallet and Nails",'
They joked, hammering,
'Drinkers at Death's cup,
Leaves hanging off a dead tree.'
Then hoisted us, a pitiless exhibit,
To writhe together,
     hanging between earth and air,
Comrades on the gibbet of the sky.

You might not choose
To share such anguish with a stranger
But I would have chosen these,
And slung between them
Shared the hours it took to die.

Friends who had walked with me fled
     and left me naked.
But these two, tied and skewered
With me, shared their bleak humanity.
     One cursed his fate
     and mocked my helplessness.

I heard him, raging at a God
Who stood aloof from all the grievance of his life,
Not knowing that I bled
    alongside always. Eternity
Will quieten all his raving disbelief.

The other turned
    and gave me all he had, his pain
    and broken hopes,
Called me by name and fixed his eyes of agony
    on mine.
He shared the hours of darkness with me,
Reminded me of why I came
As thirst and pain consumed all thought
And prayer deserted me. He
Befriended me, despite
The ultimate aloneness of our dying.

I waited for him. Led him laughing
Into light, into the green
Garden, by the quiet paths,
The sweet water,
Beneath the shade of trees
    of never-failing leaf.

Words

His mother stood watching with the other women,
Throughout the aching hours of that day,
But she alone could remember
The tearing agony of his birth,
His first cry,
The cloths with which she wound him.
Just as now they had brought cloths
To enfold his body after death
And give him rest.
Perhaps she remembered that cry as she heard him
Cry out that all was completed now, both
Coming from that searing place in the lungs.
The first from the abandoning of the womb,
The gasp of air, and now this the great conclusion
     of his life,
The entry into the eternal, the preface to the return
To his Father.
She might have heard it as a cry whose ripples
     would spread out
As those stirred by a pebble tossed into the water,
Spreading out and out beyond sight,
Disturbing currents in the depths,

And now travelling out beyond hearing
To fill and resonate the furthest corners
Of the universe.

She would have heard all words
Spoken from the pinnacle of the cross and seen
   their meaning,
Their coherence. The forgiveness, the promise of Paradise,
The thirst (poignant reminder of his infant dependence
   on her),
The agony of the cry of abandonment,
That most human cry of alienation and distress
When even Fatherhood seems silent.
But before that, those moments of intimacy
And provision.
John had somehow dared to return
And stood beside her, watching with her,
And it was to them Jesus spoke: your son, your mother,
That neither should be alone to carry the burden of grief
Or fear the future. And in so doing
He spoke prophetically of a renewed community,
An uncomplicated priority
Of love and relationship across generations,
Across gender and age and all diversity, the epitome

Of what should be called church.
She heard his words, and now within the sheltering arm
Of John, his words and even the slow
Agonising process of her Son's death became bearable.
She remembered other words, 'My time has not yet come',
And knew their meaning. And then
After he surrendered his spirit, she saw the water and
   the blood
Pour from his side, and all things became one:
His birth, his death. She remembered angels
And shepherds, and the strange wise men coming
   from the East,
And the flight to Egypt.
And now this: soon, soon, they would take him down
From the cross, wrenching out the nails and wrapping him
With tenderness, and laying him in a tomb.
Beyond that she was not sure, but she knew
It would be wonderful.
Weeping now, enduring for a night of bewildering
And devastating loss,
But, mysteriously, not without hope
That radiant joy would come in the morning.

The Sabbath Day

SATURDAY

The earth waits,
Lapis and silver
Hanging amidst circling stars,
Its canyon depths and mountain shoulders
Crinkled like tissue.
Fragile with distance.

As the full tide swells trembling
Before the ebb compels
                its fall,
Or at the lowest margin of the shore
A fringe of delicate and powerless surf
Holds like an indrawn breath
Before the surge begins again.

Or as the bare field,
Plough-ribbed, searched and scoured by winter,
Releases sudden luminous blades of green –
A velvet nap caught in a trick of light,
Long before the spring.

So the earth waits.
Between tides,
Between seasons,
Between tomb and garden.

FATHOMS

The decompression of a sealed chamber.

> Stillness, and the hours fall like leaves,
> Limbs loosen from years of fathoming mortality.
> Cells stretch into huger life.

A day passes as a thousand years.

> Remembered, that first of all confinements,
> And the forced narrowing of birth.
> Love, joy, anguish, sorrow, apprehended
> Within the strangely heavy garb of flesh.

> All paths walked then with seeming leaden feet:
> The deeps of unexplored and darkened caverns
> Or the vertiginous heights
> Forgotten
> Since that first exhilaration of creation.

The eyes' ageless penetration
Now blinkered
Within the heavy helmet of the head.

Awaiting now the huge hilarity of resurrection,
Rising light and light to laughter
Within unfettered elements of space and air.

PIERCINGS

Teacher, Inspector, a restless class.
I had been advised. 'Go easy on him.
They're a difficult lot to manage
And she's quite capable of wrecking his plans altogether.
Loud. Can't wait to get out. He's doing his best
To pull them through the syllabus before the exam.
You'll spot her straightaway. And the rest.'

So I have sympathy as he struggles
To take them through the story of an ancient passion,
Sufferings and betrayal new as today,
Stumbling at horror,
Wondering at a daybreak two days after.

'So where' (he was sweating) 'd'you think
He went, what was he doing, those hours
After death and burial?'

The silence lasts for aeons.

His eyes flicker hopefully to the front,
The predictable tryers.

The class stirs and shuffles, sighs.
Shrugs its corporate body.

Girl with piercings
Of lips and brow,
Black-nailed tips to fingers, hair spiked into thorns.
Jumper ragged over wrists to hide the slashes.
Her hand, raised. 'Sir.
Sir.'
I see his trapped eyes shift. The door, the window,
The front row. Nothing.
'Sir.'

'Yes, Della?' (O God, no, he begs)
'That's easy, innit,' she says.
'He went to Hell to find his friend Judas.
He'd lost his friend. He went to find him.'

An indrawn breath.
Theology rocks.

Girl, Goth. Moth at the candle of self-harm,
Just so He will find you, even in its flame.

ON the First Day of the Week

WONDER

Why, I ask, as countless others must
Have asked, why the writer's diligence
To emphasise
The cloth rolled up and separated
From the winding cloths that seemed to hold his body?
Was it the angels,
Having ground back the quern of stone
That closed the tomb,
Was it their awed impatience to see his face
(Known and beloved before)
And see how mortality had marred it?
And as they entered, did they say,
As he once said,
'Wake up', or like the trumpet of the war horse
Shout, 'Come forth'?
Surely their touch, however loving
And devoted, was not needed.
This Man could rise through winding,
Swaddling cloths of burial,
Material being now to him immaterial,
Free to move through doors and distance.

Perhaps they brought spring water
To wash away the blooded lacerations
Of his brow, or, like Mary, wept to see
And washed him with angelic tears?
We cannot know. Perhaps such tenderness
In love would be unbearable for us to glimpse
Constrained as we are by our humanity.
But this we do know: there is no mention
Of that shameful mockery of a crown.
His hands and feet and side, yes,
But not the pierced and bruised brow.

Those thorns have borne no fruit,
Nor is there any harvest rising here
From the bitterness of wanton cruelty.
Only the true harvest of the risen bread,
Broken and shared to nurture broken lives.

RESURRECTION

THOMAS

I was not there: I fled and hid.
Grief and bewilderment crouched me
In a space
In the crook of a tree. I waited
Until I could no longer bear to be alone.

They told me that he walked through doors
As if through air, spoke to them,
Forgave their desertion, laughed
With them about their incredulity,
Then vanished.
I could not believe, excluded
From their joyous certainties
And yet unable to turn away and leave.

Waiting, for I knew not what,
My questions hardened: show me
Flesh and blood, the Man I knew,
The grasp of that hand, the terrible evidence
Of scars. No ghost, no apparition
Moving soundlessly through walls and doors.

Do not judge my doubts and questions:
They are for you, as for me,
The footprints that will lead you
To the greatest revelation.

TRAVELLING

Our road cut between ash grey hills,
Blurring as the sun collapsed to the west.
Our feet were urgent, desperate for home,
Yet stumbling with the dread of a cold hearth,
The morning's bread dry,
The wine sour in a shrunken wineskin.
We talked, words half-expressed,
Thoughts unformed, as though
There were no true words left, no coherent Word,
Fragments only. Companions, shoulder to shoulder,
Yet alone, bewildered, in the separateness of grief.
Sometimes, a pang of hope, from the absurdity
Of the morning's news, but
Always the undertow of disbelief.
We did not hear the following footsteps
Scuffing the dust, hurrying to overtake us,
Until the voice spoke,

Questions, as though we had been overheard
In all our doubts and sadness.
A stranger to us, whose patient answers
Turned slowly to brimming laughter
At our bafflement,
Our incredulity.

*

He came with us, our fellow-traveller,
To share our paucity of hospitality.
We recognised him then, as the stale bread broke,
Transformed to blessing in the vibrant hands.

DAYBREAK

Gently, she let her footsteps take her back
To yesterday, leaving the household sleeping,
Scoured by grief but burnished now with joy.
The dark sky, splintered with stars, waited
For the sun to run a burning finger
Along the rim of the earth.
Trees whispered of their guardianship of time.
Then, a sudden rush of shimmering brightness,
Birdsong, and a shivering breeze.

Here, at the maw of rock,
She had flung her desperate question,
And heard it answered.
Here she had been named, known,
As in a pristine moment, God had so named Adam.
Then Adam, Woman,
While creatures gathered to them, to receive
Each marvellous identity.
She, too, had found her true self, named and called
To endless possibility.

The earth, silver and green and gold,
Had sprung afresh to life. New made. Unfurled.

That daybreak, beneath ancient trees
Rooted in springs deeper than memory,
She saw how Resurrection bathes the world in light,
Healing its age-embittered wounds and shames.
This radiance will transform its weariness,
Quicken its people to eternal playfulness,
Their garden-given innocence restored.

Riddle

I am road and traveller.

Darkest-before-dawn waiting
And the once-glimpsed star, flying
In shreds of cloud.

I am word and silence,
Shout and whisper,
Storm-sleeper, wave-walker.

I am tree and carpenter.
I turn the tables and rebuild the house.

I am rock and feather
And the falling sparrow.

I am the naked truth.

Sources and Acknowledgements

Scripture quotations are from the New Revised Standard Version Bible, copyright © 1989 National Council of the Churches of Christ in the United States of America. Used by permission. All rights reserved worldwide.

Some of these poems appeared previously in *The Road Chosen*, by Janet Killeen, Wild Goose Publications, *Wilderness*, a Wild Goose download, and in various Wild Goose anthologies.